lrony Of Dreams

OrangeBooks Publication

Smriti Nagar, Bhilai, Chhattisgarh - 490020

Website: **www.orangebooks.in**

First Edition, 2021

ISBN: 978-93-92878-07-7

Feels Like The Stars Are Near

Irony of Dreams

Proggayan Banerjee
Kuroba Hareta

Powered By
Dream Planner Event
Management & Manpower Sol.

OrangeBooks Publication

www.orangebooks.in

Table Of Contents

➤ **Society Impropriety** 1

    I Dream 2

    Caste 4

    Irony...6

    God 10

    The Therapist 12

    Is It Right?...14

➤ **The Life**..**16**

    Datebayo 17

    Bro 20

    Façade...22

    My Obscurity 25

    Jobless...27

    Again And Again.................................29

    Reality...31

    I Won't Leave.....................................33

- **Irony of Love** **35**
  - Confessions 36
  - The Boy Who I Loved 38
  - Why Is It So?...40
  - I Wish..42
  - One More Chance..44
  - Notice Me Senpai 46

- **Beauty Of Season's** **48**
  - Chilled Wishes Of A Wintry Night 49
  - Winter And Coffee Thoughts 51
  - Rain, I Feel Like I Love You 53
  - Rain, Is A Comedy 55
  - The Season I Like..57

Society Impropriety

I Dream

The world is full of crazy games ,
Crazy people and annoying names.
You are born With so emence joy;
Yet at the end of the day you are just a toy.
Being a boy thought it is easy to be a girl;
But later realized its the human nature
to get yourself in the swirl.
Bit by bit started to learn and gain,
Yet at the end it's just a word "PAIN".

I dream of a world where the sun is bright ;
Where people are free and can sleep tight .
The place I dream Is a beautiful place
Where there are no thief's to be chased.
But here it comes the dreadful fate
It's just a dream and nothing to relate .
The dream is over and the truth is here,
Another day, " I need to go but where".

It feel's like I am lost;
In the desserts of my thoughts ,
I know that I am scribbling ,
Please try to read without giggling.
But these thoughts are deep and tough to neglect
Though I know this is just the game of fate.
Now , it feels like I am loosing it all
All that matters is that will I Rise or Fall.

Now I get it , What's happening to me !
The dreams just disturbing cause it comes free.
Whereas the real world is tough
with misery's and sorrows;
Even this life of ours is being borrowed.
I promise myself not to dream from now
Or people will say, " Are you a Donkey or a cow?"
Speaking of cow's, now I dream again;
Yet at the end it's just a word "PAIN".

-Proggayan Banerjee

Caste

The day was beautiful and good indeed ,
Until a guy asked me in park ,
" Which religion do you bleed".
Now this is a part quite to be confused ,
Because no one has the right to chose.
You are born and labelled with the tag,
Follow it properly bro, Or they will call you a drag.

If you follow Christ, offer candle ;
There's no second choice you have to go to Bandel.
If Shiva is the one you follow, offer milk;
And if Allah is your savior give sheets of silk.
These are things that we are meant to do ,
Is these the things they really wanted from you.
I think the one who created all
Would rather say these things
to someone who might fall.

Over and over Thought what to say ,
These is a topic on which I can think for the whole day.
The guy looked curious to know my caste ,
But I really didn't knew what to
say about a topic this vast.
At last I thought of playing a game ;
And replied him by saying,
"Proggayan Banerjee is my name" .

Instantly the guy called his call,
And said , " So you are a Brahmin after all".
I smiled a bit and thought again;
He judged my tag just by the name .
Before leaving I turned to him
And noticed the guy trying to make a Hymn;
I smiled and said , "Brahmin's not my caste
I believe in HUMANITY above all,
Cause there nothing else I can trust."

- Proggayan Banerjee

Irony

*Given the numbers, every year 700,000+
people kill themselves;
But these are only the ones that are reported,
There are also unreported accidents;
And bodies so obscure, that were never escorted.
Millions of attempts fail,
Instead of sending them to therapist, they're send to jail.
Also, don't forget the fine you'd pay,
Which might be almost half of your remaining wealth,
It's such a great way to improve your mental health.*

*But hey, how can I be so salty,
I live in such a great country.
Where elections are considered ,essential';
But education's not.
Well, it never was in the first place,
It was like a step child of the Human Rights;
Being gifted an old shoe with a torn lace.*

But, to be fair, this system was mocked
enough by a British guy named Dave,
So, I'll let education slither in its little cave.

What I adore of my nation,
Are its flower politicians.
Be it social media or the news,
They're always drawing views,
They're screwing us forever, we claim,
but we won't let 'em lose,
Because even it's a democracy,
We're too lazy to choose.

Yes we're lazy most of the times,
But not when we want to try;
Government formation isn't a big deal,
Do you know what is? To stop being a guy kissing a guy.
Gay Is Not A Gender,
It's A Damn Disease;
Get In The Line Or You'll Be Deceased!

No, not literal death, that'd be unfair,
Instead you'll be married to your
dad's friend's daughter.

Do you know the word ,,sex'? Of course, you've
all seen the leaked private motel tapes.
We're making fun of em, as we do the same for rapes;
Well why shouldn't we, rapes are all the victim's fault,
"The accused just wanted to give bodily
pleasure to a 12 year old,
It was her fault to revolt."
That's what goes on in the courts,
When the victim dares to report,
Even if it's a satire, the last couple
of lines weren't jokes.

"But what about those two and a half
cases where justice was served?"
Do you really believe those were the
only ones who deserved?

Because I know there's million other cases,
Whose parents earn less than minimum waged,
So instead the-rapist gets a reward,
Gets to „pleasure" the victim as an award,
For keeping it a secret untold.

But hey, our nation has some serious unity,
Remember us getting offended by a joke by PewDiePie?
It was fun to see all of us whine and cry;
"Wait, for attention, you're supporting a racist guy?"
Well yea, the whole satire's for attention,
But at least I don't go on asking momo's
to every visible North-East guy.

But I guess seeking attention is bad,
Trust me though, I'm a good guy;
I do charity, don't I?

Kuroba Hareta

God

Seven Continents, countless religions;
Signs of peace are fucking pigeons.
Been suffering from a lot of grieve?
Thank your sexy momma Eve!

Savior he is, he truly is;
Don't believe me? Just ask some terrorists.
You did something nice? He sure has been guiding you,
Done something wrong? Buddy, that's you.

Well if someone kills your parents, forgive him;
You told a lie? Too bad, your afterlife seems dim.
Be enslaved to him, you get promoted
to be a heavenly one;
If you don't I'm sorry, but Hell is your only destination.

Epidemic and Disasters? Those are Satan's crap;
What's the Almighty doing? I'm sorry,
but He's taking a nap.
Rape your wife, since you own that bitch;
Kiss your lover? Dude that snitch got a serious stitch.

Tired of your life, realizing you won't ever shine?
If you gonna suicide, gotta tell you
that's your sin to our Divine.
Prayed to Him asking stuffs? Damn, you're greedy;
Didn't pray? Well my friend that's why you're needy.

Stop using your brains, be enslaved to his "Word",
The "Almighty Savior" whom you call GOD.

-Kuroba Hareta

The Therapist

A child went to therapy,
He had been mentally stressed for a while.
The child saw a man of his father's age,
With a hearty big smile.
"Welcome Sammy", the therapist said,
"I heard you're good at rapping."
"Yes" replied Sammy. "Show me some", said the man.
Sammy began to drop his rhymes, while
on the table, the therapist kept tapping.
"We do make good music, don't we?", said Mr. Bob,
"How about we start a band."
Slowly Sammy became comfortable,
Playing many raps hand in hand.

Few months later, Sammy's depression went away,
It's due time to stop the therapy,
The two made their last song,
As for his departure, Sammy got ready.
4 days later Mr. Bob was found dead in his apartment,
Seems like he was depressed as well.
Sammy, his last client, was the one keeping
him sane, but now that he was gone,
Things weren't anymore well.
I wonder if Sammy got know,
What happened to his mate.
Sometimes it's quite wild things,
That is being planned by fate.

-Kuroba Hareta

Is It Right?

Is it right when you want someone and don't get them,
Is it right to cry on their name .
Is it right to hurt someone ;
With the sword for words the work is done.
Is it right to judge the cover of a book,
And call someone a whore just by the look.

Is it write to discriminate
So that people loose their faith .
Is it right to ask the question's which I do ;
Cause people ask me what is it to you.

No i just can be like the people around
And eventually no one will stop to
pick you from the ground.

I think "It Is Right" to do all this
But is this humanity someone describe please.
The world is deep and tough to get,
This current world is the real thing to hate .
If things like "these" are right to do ;
I would better die and later see you.

-Proggayan Banerjee

The Life

Datebayo

Let's hear the tale of a boy
Who thought will have all the joy.
The kid was 16 and had to earn
That was of course not out of fun.
It was cause he had to read,
And be the best man he could ever be.
Started searching but got none
But finally got the job for his run.

The work is easy as it seems ;
You just had to call and say,
"Give me 2 minutes please".
Slowly and slowly learned how to take call,
Now my speech was better so that people can fall.
The company was genuine and legit indeed ;
All you needed to do was ask everything
from his D.O.B TO FUNEREAL DEED.
But this is not all for it ,
Cause there were targets to be hit.

No matter how hard I tried to get
But eventually had to wait ;
It started to seem it's not meant for me ,
It will be better if I see something else better to be .
Lost with self everyday I ask ;
"Why do I have to smile just like the Mask".
Sitting alone a day I thought
Let's leave hope and there's nothing to be fought ;

Suddenly buzzed my phone, as I saw;
It was my team lead Mr. Shaw.
I picked the phone and heard him say,
"You are coming tomorrow at day"
The question strike the storm in me ,
Is it my conscience talking to me ;
I wanted to ask him what should I do,
Instead I said , " Yes I will call you".

I think he guessed what's going on
And said before ending , " Everything
will be fine tomorrow just carry on".
The words left deep and propounding for me
And I said before ending, " Thanks , Let's see".
My blood rushed like never before ,
I now had to see how far can I go.
Bit by bit I learned everyday ,
As days passed by there were a lot of things I could say.

My targets where slowly coming up ;
Is it because I fought so tough ?
The way was tough and rough to get,
But the key is to never give up and wait.
That is the reason I say , " Get up and try",
To know your worth and get yourself high;
And , " Never give up until you get,
So that later there is nothing to regret".

-Proggayan Banerjee

Bro

I remember some things of days that good ,
When their was no tension to have food
I was the youngest of the two
And I remember my brother teasing and
saying me , "Hey who are you?"
I and my bro were the best of all
Neither of us would let the other fall.

Like other siblings fighting was a disease,
And I liked everything he did
from eating bread to cheese .
Our fights started everyday we what to see,
I said "Takeshi's castle" and he said "Na, Na chi".
The fight was usually long and intense
Yet at the end we did everything
together which made no sense .

I liked the way we played ,
I like the way we quarreled everyday .
Things were going so great ,
Until I began growing till date.
Now things are different from what they were
Its a bit difficult cause I don't stay here .

Probably this is just time that has turned the table,
Eventually no one will be there to make you stable.
My brother and I now stay far away,
We meet every week just for a day.
I know its my fault and I shouldn't say;
I was the one who chose to step out of the bay .

But still I believe "Brother's are by heart",
No matter what happens I will be there if you get hurt.
I think I should have told him but no,
"I had and will always love you my bro"

-Proggayan Banerjee

Façade

Hey, bear with this "poem" without a rhyme,
Let me get through my feelings just this time.
Is it okay to not be strong, is it okay to have a dream
When you know you won't get them
"It's not good chasing something that doesn't exist"
So you mean I should just live without a goal
An empty vessel?
If you think I'm writing this to beg for
your attention, you're indeed right,
I'm such a sore loser!
Regardless, I am lucky to be handed everything
And unlucky to be getting them snatched away,
As if they weren't ever mine!
I can't complain, can I?
But let's get into the present, what I have.

To be precise I have everything,
except my dreams and you;
I don't know why it ended the way it did
It's not your fault, it's always been mine,
Always will be mine.
B-but I can't take this anymore
Do I really deserve this
Why me? Why it had to be me?
Please if possible come back.
I can planned to say a million
"fuck you"s in this poem
But I couldn't
It's your fault, hehe.
I know I won't get a chance.
I know I don't deserve one.
But I can't really move on.
Is it over? Should I disintegrate?
If I do, if I really do
Please, I hope you don't forget me,
Because how many times may I say
"I don't give a damn"

But I love you.
Living with such a foolish reason is so me
I don't know, how long can I last, hehe.
I'm sorry to everyone who believe in me
Also to everyone who pretend to love me
Sorry to every stranger
Sorry to every friends
But don't worry(or rather hold my burden)
Because this is not a suicide note, or is it?
Regardless I love funerals.
I hope they play "21 Guns" or "Boulevard
of Broken Dreams" in mine
Sorry for being immature throughout, but I'm 19
Regardless this is what I-
Hahaha, did you all think I was serious?
I was just kidding!
Maybe naming this cringefest "Façade" shall be fitting.
-The person behind Kuroba Hareta

My Obscurity

I'm almost 20 when I'm writing this shit,
People have expectations
Of great achievements, or that I'll never quit,
Or take of care of all situations.

They revere me,
Portraying me as someone without flaws;
Or they pity me,
Like without tusks are our pair of jaws.

I don't know, where I exist now
There's this loop I'm living over and over again;
I have no clue of the way to stop being in sunlight now,
And the next moment in heavy rain.

Is it weird for me to cry?
Is it weird to get furious?
Does my history just makes my humanity defy?
All these questions make me curious.

Why I can't I just behave like a kid like others my age?
After all I'm 20 when I'm writing this.
Will my life be the cost of my stockpiled rage?
My air-castle keeps me sane, while
I stay on the border of abyss.

-Kuroba Hareta

Jobless

Being jobless I thought will find something else ,
But little did I know about the place .
It is foolish to think ;
That not even once have you blink .
No one care's what you did before ,
If you can't afford now they can even call you a whore .
Earned a lot and wasted more,
Yet at the end its just a past door.
When I had a job people loved me ;
Not because of me but cause the money people see.
Had huge friend group and forum ;
And then finally all disappeared because of this norm.
I lost the job and people closest,
This is how the world works from south to west.

Here at the end being alone ,
NO one is even going to grant you a loan.
I left the job because I had dream,
Later realized , it's the real world and not a fake cream.
People need to see the note to respect you ;
Otherwise people give a fuck and who are you.
It feels like no one is here in my fate of sorrow,
This life is full of lane's narrow.
Never did I thought this would come to me
I guess it's the epitome of nature to be .
Here at the end I am just scribbling line ;
Even I think it's useless to have ,
rather for someday to shine .

-Proggayan Banerjee

Again And Again

I want to get hit by a truck and not die,

I want to sit in a room whole week and just cry..

Surrounded by people, I still feel alone,

Like an ungrateful bitch, creating this
cloak of arrogance I've worn.

For a while I thought I failed
everyone's expectations already,

But they're all coming back suddenly

And with those, accompanies new insecurities;

Feeling of a million pities,

Where am I in life at this moment?

Do I deserve to be here?

Or this will obliterate like every other figment?

This makes me dead scared.

I wish I'd make better decisions in life,
I can't even move when I'm holding
my left wrist near a knife.
,,Cause lately I've been growing weaker and weaker
Which makes me realize I might
be just an attention seeker,
And I'm starting to hate myself,
My own presence, makes me suffocate myself.
I wanna forget everything that I had been;
But when I think I have, my brain showcases
a flashback of everything I've seen.
I hope that there is a last day,
When I stop running away,
But I still fail, even if I try a lot
There's always an inch to which I'd come short.

-Kuroba Hareta

Reality

Being a kid I wondered how the stars glow
How trains work and how does someone
become a foe.
Grew a bit and wondered all about the sky
And repeatedly asked the question, "Is it that high".
Time never stops, so did I grow.
By the end I feel this life is a comedy show.
Being a boy I knew it is tough to be
And become the bright bud which you want to see
I remember back then seventeen was my age
Like others all I wanted was to be free of the cage
But little did I know the world in real,
Crying and suffering are things ideal.
Being free I get,
Welcome to reality ,there's no one to wait
The people by you have suddenly disappeared
It's only me and no one's here
Step by step I started to learn

The basics of the real fun.
The fun started with heartache and pain
And later it only started to gain.
Everyday was like an unknown way
Didn't know where to go and stay
No mom, no dad to check you well
People give a fuck and say , Man please go to hell
I miss those days when I loved to play
And doing crazy stuffs all by the day.
No tension; no pressure
Slept tight with leisure
But things are changed, there things to be tought.
Rather I need to earn so that things can be brought
I think this is the way the world works
Being a kid it's me who didn't knew the marks
Those days where good and the best of my life
Those are the memories For Rest of the time

-Proggayan Banerjee

I Won't Leave

I don't know what is wrong with me
Why do I see dreams, which are
Not meant to be
I want to become a writer for free,
I want people to know me,
I want to do what I like to do
Not for money ofcourse
Cause I enjoy the work too.
But it's not possible my boy
Cause if you don't have money there's no joy
Said a friend, 'Go, work in the firm you were".
But I really know that place
Is just for frustration and despair.
I think there's no point of writing this things,
I think this is the only way it seems

Whether I am ready to go and say,
Give me 2 minutes please.
Back to the stage where I was,
Taking non-stop calls and it was all a fuss.
Well, I don't say that the job is bad
Ultimately at some point
It was the only thing that I had
But it's just that I started to think
And the thought have kept me busy,
So that I don't even get time to blink
Still, No matter what my thoughts say,
If I have you reading this lines
I will keep writing for the whole day.
But still this world isn't just a game
I have and will always want to see
"Proggayan Banerjee as the Author Name".

-Proggayan Banerjee

Irony Of Love

Confessions

The game of confessions isn't as easy
as the "Kaguya Sama" show,

It's a lot more, "Will you be my forever or no?"

Let's start with girls, they don't confess,

The most generous thing they can do is say "YES!".

Speaking of yeses, let's start with it,

Don't forget before you hear that,
you've to kneel in defeat.

It doesn't have a guarantee though,

You may hear, "Feelings change", "You
don't love me as before", "I didn't want to
hurt you, so I said yes", so and so.

Now, there are types of rejections you can get,

Let's just get the common one, "I JUST
WANT YOU TO BE MY FRIEND!"

Yea all you male readers must be
tearing up nostalgia, right?

It was at this moment the boys start the infamous,
"NEVER GONNA GIVE YOU UP" fight.

Then maybe you might be in love with that girl
you met in a public place on a random day,

Too bad you never met her again, to
tell her what you've to say.

Facebook let's you meet this girl online,

You chat a lot, and she looks fine.

You confessed her thinking the feelings mutual,

Too bad mate, that's one less friend you had virtual.

But then isn't the worst she could do is deny?

Not really, "I need time" which she
forgets and you go on to try.

So, are all boys and girls same?

No they sometimes switch their roles in this game.

There are rare cases though,

Where confesses work as Chandler's
from "F.R.I.E.N.D.S" T.V. show.

-Kuroba Hareta

The Boy Who I Loved

I guess it's been 2 years or so ,
Now that person is my foe.
I guess I knew what happened then,
Everything I tried at that was in vain .
I loved him, He loved me
And this is the thing people of this world couldn't see.

Yes! I am a boy and I loved a guy,
Does that mean I should go and die.
I really want to know what is wrong with me ;
Guys like girls but I really loved him unconditionally .

Is that my fault to love him which I do
It seems like the comments people passed ,
Where more important to you.
You promised me we cold fight till the end

And ultimately Would make those people bend .
Else I am just here scribbling line ,
And when people ask , "How are you"
I say , "Oh! I am fine."

NO I am not fine for god's Sake ,
Dont you remember those nights or was it all fake ;
I understand you had nothing to do
It happened because of what people said to you .
" You are a boy and it's disgusting to
have a boyfriend" - said his friend
I know how it feels Cause I have
also heard them at the end.
You said , " My groups teasing me , I can't handle",
Eventually I have also dealt with those type of scoundrel.
I think I know what's disturbing me ,
I tried everything I could,
Its just that you couldn't see .

-Proggayan Banerjee

Why Is It So?

I know you must hate me, must regret knowing,
Wishing the guy never texted me to say 'Hi' to you.
You think I regret the same,
After all the shit we've been through.
I won't take the blame anymore,
It feels lame that I'm the loser in a single player game,
I understand you hate, and you're not a tsundere,
But tell me, when I don't text you for a week,
Why do you text me, just to fight me?
Is it necessary to hurt me?
Is it necessary to be good with me, only
to leave again the next day?
Because darling you call it harassment, when
I ask you the reason for something,
But tell me, am I always wrong?
You asked me a question today, and
I asked you one through that;

Why can't I give you up? Maybe because, I feel like,
Falling in love with someone else would make me......
But, that's what you think what I am, a slut!
So I know you hate it, but,
I swear darling, if you're reading this,
this is the last poem about us,
I need some answers to some questions I have;
What is it that makes you think, I'm what you say?
Darling, tell me do you really think I'm pretending
everything just to fuck you one day?
The fact is, that, yes, I do. I do. I do want to have sex,
But you're chastity isn't what I'm after,
You just happened to be the perfect girl,
the perfectest girl that ever could be.
And I want to be with you, cheesy as it is,
I don't want to harass you anymore,
Darling, babe, I'm sorry for being the one,
But why is it so difficult to fall out of love with you.

– Kuroba Hareta

I Wish

Okay! So this is a topic I am not good with,
Fortunately "love" Is a subject every teenagers say it .
" I love you"; "Will you marry me" is it all;
I don't understand just by hearing
this how can someone fall.
Definition of " love" is tough to get
For someone it 's an emotion and someone it 's a Date.
Got tired of searching the real meaning of love
And suddenly as I saw a couple , I knew it was a bluff.
They said , "Babu, shona " and sat beside each other
But all I saw them doing was hovering over the phone ;
And watching the either from top to the tower 's.

I asked myself is this called love to have
If this is the thing Then I shall never have
At last, I thought of going back
I guess „Love"is a thing
I will always lack
But then I thought again
„will I even know the meaning of love?
Or I am just trying in vain
„Love is word which is tough to get
Also it is always followed by „Regret"

-Proggayan Banerjee

One More Chance

My life is shamble of stupid words ,
Can I make it go?
I didn't expect to be an idiot like this,
On the years that I used to grow.
Hey, I'm wondering why is it so hard to talk,
I know all roses have thorn,
The world says we're incompatible,
Like you being a Gemini and me a Capricorn.
You say I don't follow my own positive outlook,
But you can't compare a grape to a flower :
One stays beautifully, enhancing the scenery,
While the other is something that
leaves its consumer sour.

I understand I say hurtful things that have no apology,
And yes I do deserve to be alone.
But for me, only me, give me another last chance.
I swear I won't be taking it as a granted one.
I know we won't be together forever,
It's not a fairy tale
But don't end it this way
Let us give our ship a shot to sail.
Which I'm sure is to sink
Leaving a bad scratch.
That's why I wrote this,
Instead of checking if we're an ideal match.
I'm Sorry. .

-Kuroba Hareta

Notice Me Senpai

Frick all the psychopathic and depressing
poems and be ready to blush,

WHY?

Cuz this poem is a wholesome one to make you,

NOTICE ME SENPAI!!!!!!!

It wasn't love at first sight, like
those pesky fuckboy suckas,

It was our conversations that
made me fall for you BAKA!!!

I liked u since highschool.

"M-me? I-I like you too!!!"

I heard you say that in my dream last night,

Where in a most romantic way, I said "I love you"!!!!!

I still remember when you were high,

You wanted to eat

You texted me at night,
I got so excited, I threw my phone YEET!!!!
Hey I'm kinda broke,
But I can still make you my queen;
All you have to do in this hearts' battle,
Is give me the win.
Hey let's meet sometime and
watch some Sitcoms together,
And definitely not hentai!
But that's only my fantasy,
Until you notice me senpai.
Now for the readers of this poem,
Who think my style is kinda wrong;
In my defense I tried to mimic;
The style of a K-Pop song.

-Kuroba Hareta

Beauty Of Season's

Chilled Wishes Of A Wintry Night

Winter and romance, does sound like oxymorons,
After all the painters and poets; they
portray it as a melancholy somber;
Whereas as rains and springs,
"help" grow flowers from thorns,
And summers are portrayed as a shining amber.

As I unfurl my blanket's foldings,
I couldn't veto more to the opinion
that winter makes us lonely.
Winter love can be as wild as Summer, if not more,
Because the warmth of someone's
touch, is all we long for;
I, for myself, want my first love making be in winter,
Millions of times have I fancied being pampered
by someone's touch in late November;
But people say Monsoon's better,
it makes them extra wet,

Go ahead y'all, laugh your bottoms out,
the pun here was intended.

Fancies, sarcasm, needs and kinks aside,
Winters do feel lonely inside,
End of romances and broken vows,
Freezes on our skin now,
Love freezes, so does sorrow,,
While some escape and sleep desiring to
be awakened on a better tomorrow;
Others sit with a cup of coffee, in their heart's solitary,
Inspecting for the fanciest words in their vocabulary,
Canvasing winter and romance as an oxymoron,
With no warmth to provide other
than some lovers"scorn.

-Kuroba Hareta

Winter And Coffee Thoughts

Hey, people are wearing baggy clothes;
Maybe I won't look too fat anymore,
Well at least for the rest of this year.
The yellow leaves have fallen,
Fogs are getting thicker,
It's tougher to navigate with glasses dear.

Hey, maybe you guys think, ,,He's fat and all'',
,,He doesn't even feel cold, it's just
better than summer for him!

But trust me, I'm freezing;
Because my skin is unfortunately
made up of same stuff as yours"
So yea if I spend a lot of time in the wintry fog;
I'll damn sure be sneezing.

But the a cup or two of warm coffee comes to the save,
Making me like a bear resting in its cave.

I wonder if someone feels the same?
Maybe not; As my winter thoughts are just lame.

-Kuroba Hareta

Rain, I Feel Like I Love You

We've had our differences, haven't we?
I thought you laughed at me,
thinking my life as a comedy.
I'd despise you, wish for you to go away,
Now that I look, you've always been
the permanent one to stick with me.
In all dark times, I needed to hide my tears,
You would camouflage them by drenching me.
All the times I would need to divert my mind,
You'd roar with your lightnings.

It's like we're in a toxic relationship
You laugh at me, I hate you;
But we've been together whenever I need you.
Hey Ame or Rain or Brishti or Barish
or your uncountable names,
Drench me with you
From my hair to my toe
Kiss me with your watery lips
Let's get this toxicity out.
Now that no one's there
Now that no one cares
Be with me forever
Sink me as if you're a river,
I love you!

-Kuroba Hareta

Rain, Is A Comedy

We've had our differences, haven't we?
I thought you laughed at me,
thinking my life as a comedy.
I'd despise you, wish for you to go away,
Now that I look, you've always been
the permanent one to stick with me.
In all dark times, I needed to hide my tears,
You would camouflage them by drenching me.
All the times I would need to divert my mind,
You'd roar with your lightnings.
It's like we're in a toxic relationship
You laugh at me, I hate you;
But we've been together whenever I need you.

Hey Ame or Rain or Brishti or Barish
or your uncountable names,

Drench me with you

From my hair to my toe

Kiss me with your watery lips

Let's get this toxicity out.

Now that no one's there

Now that no one cares

Be with me forever

Sink me as if you're a river,

I love you!

-Kuroba Hareta

The Season I Like

Oh! I guess it's december
Actually I don't remember,
Cause all it has to be
Darker and cold days
Feels like is staying for eternity
Actually this seasons is like the world in real,
Dark with misery and sorrows,
Cold like things ideal
Though I like the vibe it has,
I like it because it has Christmas
I like it cause nature's beautiful
I like the way it is,
I don't know why, probably I am fool
This season has a lot of things to be told

58

„Favourite season for marriage"from days so old
Where you can see heavens in real
Rain in peculiar form, much colder,
Not like the rain in real
When you can see magics happening,
Like walking over lakes
Or even might see thanos snapping.
I think you have already guessed
So I guess there's nothing to be said
I think I am just writing cause I am a free thinker
Or may be because It is The One Only Winter.

-Proggayan Banerjee

Acknowledgement

As we come to the end
of the book, we wish to
thank some people

Firstly, Our Families

*Hell, who needs inspirations when you got family right?
That's what vin diesel said. Although as they joked
around our poems, they did support us
all throughout our journey*

Some Idiots

*So in this part we thank some of our friends, who
had to hide their cringe while reading
our early stages of poems.*

Kuroba Hareta

*I'd like to thank my inspirations, which are couple of
poets i'm lucky enough to call my friends.*

*Muntasir tuhin who criticed my works
and helped me to get better.*

Everyone involved in kuroba hareta.

Proggayan Bannerjee

*My brother, pronyt banerjee for offcourse
not reading my stuffs but still there for me*

*To all the people in flat up here who have stayed awake
for me the whole while. A special thanks to dhrubajati
mondal, abhishek naskar, rudra chakraborty, rishi
mukherjee, amrito das & dipishika gayen
for always staying there for me.*

*Lastly to the ones for who i still write and i guess my
rhymes are just the implications of all the
feelings i came to know with them; to akash.*

Our Investor

*Dream planner event management and man power sol
for making it possible for us to actually publish this
book. Alot of thanks to mr. Dhrubajyati
mondal to acccept our work.*

Our Publishers

*Thanks to orange book publications our publishers
who are helping us through our first steps of
publishing our books and fulfilling our dreams.*

*****Also Thanks To Ourselves Lol****